This Book Belongs To

____

My Birthday is: ______________________________

There are 12 signs in Astrology. They are made up of 4 Families: Fire, Water, Air and Earth. They also share special Qualities, Cardinal, Mutable and Fixed. In the Zodiac Wheel they have their own house. We are going to visit each Sign and learn how they connect to our Human Body.

The Signs of the Fire Family Aries, Leo and Sagittarius are playful, strong and courageous. Fire signs like to play and adventure.

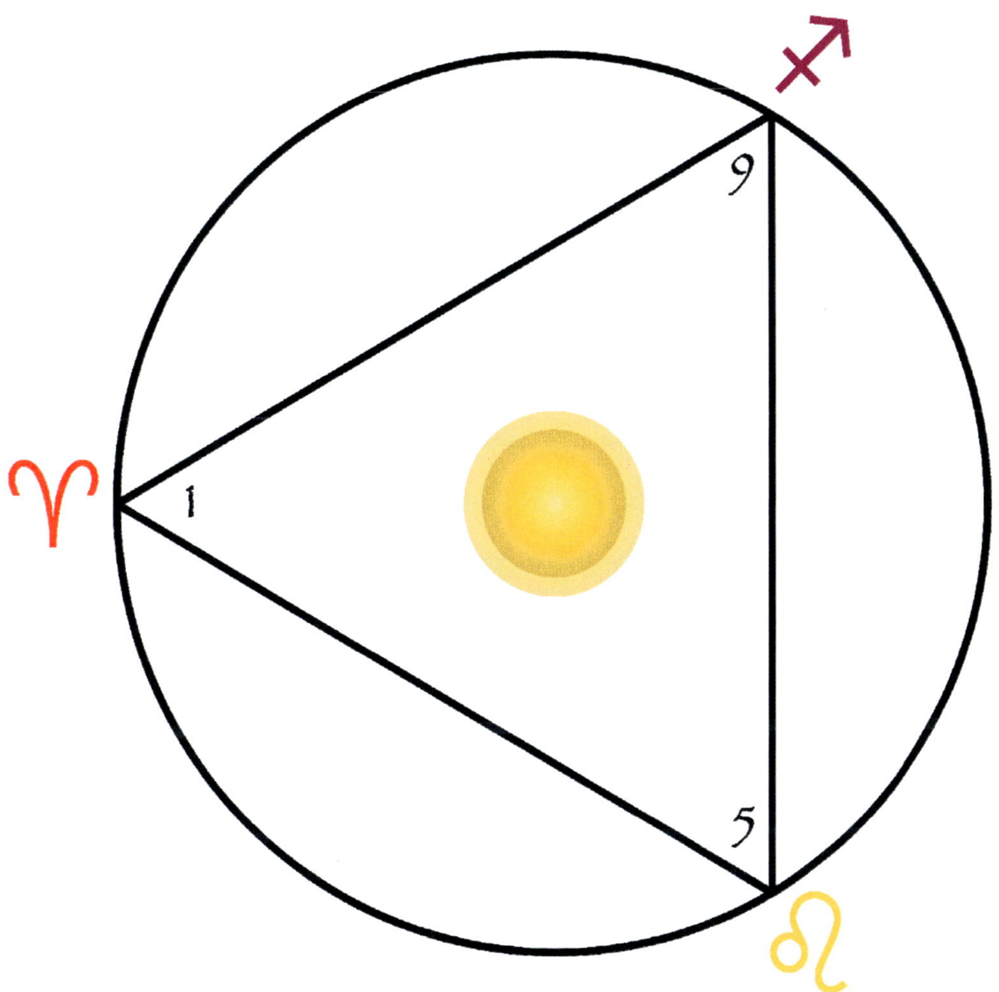

The Signs of the Earth family Capricorn, Taurus and Virgo are hardworking, tough and determined. Earth signs like to be stable and organized.

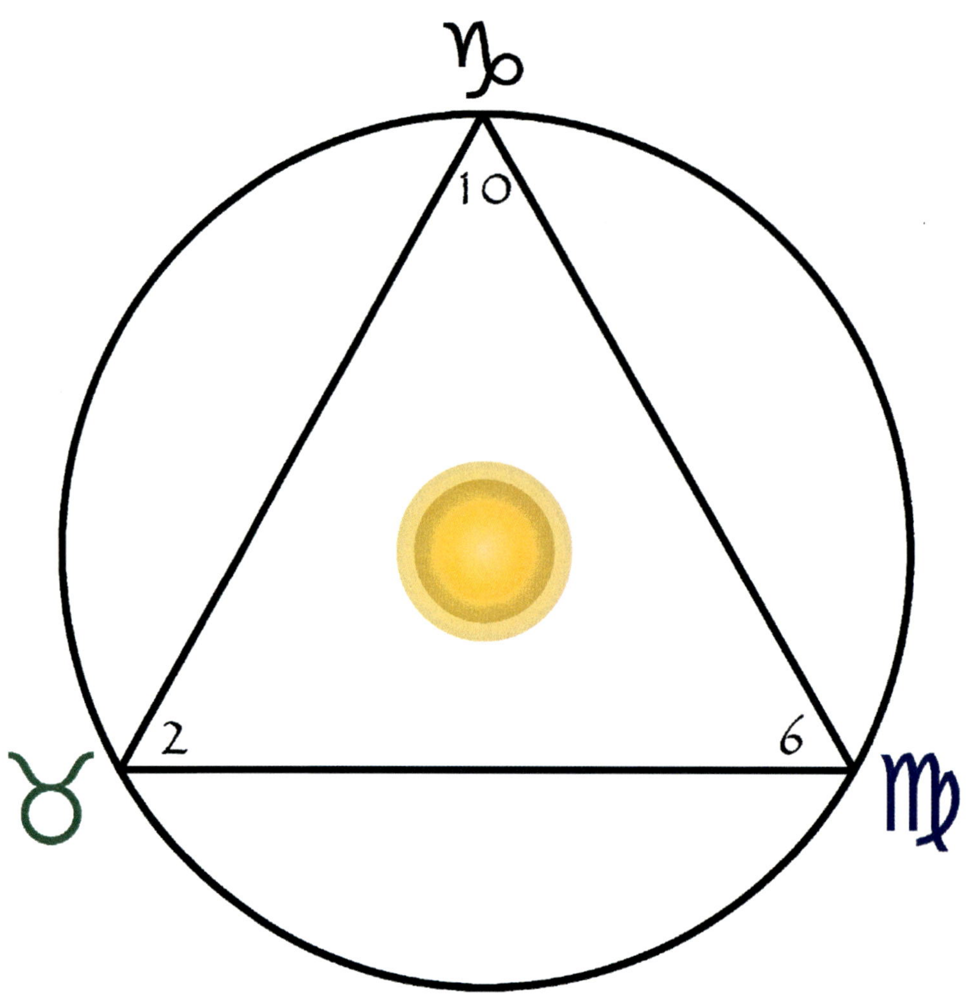

The Signs of the Air Family Aquarius, Gemini and Libra are intelligent, curious and free- spirited. Air signs like to talk and share with friends.

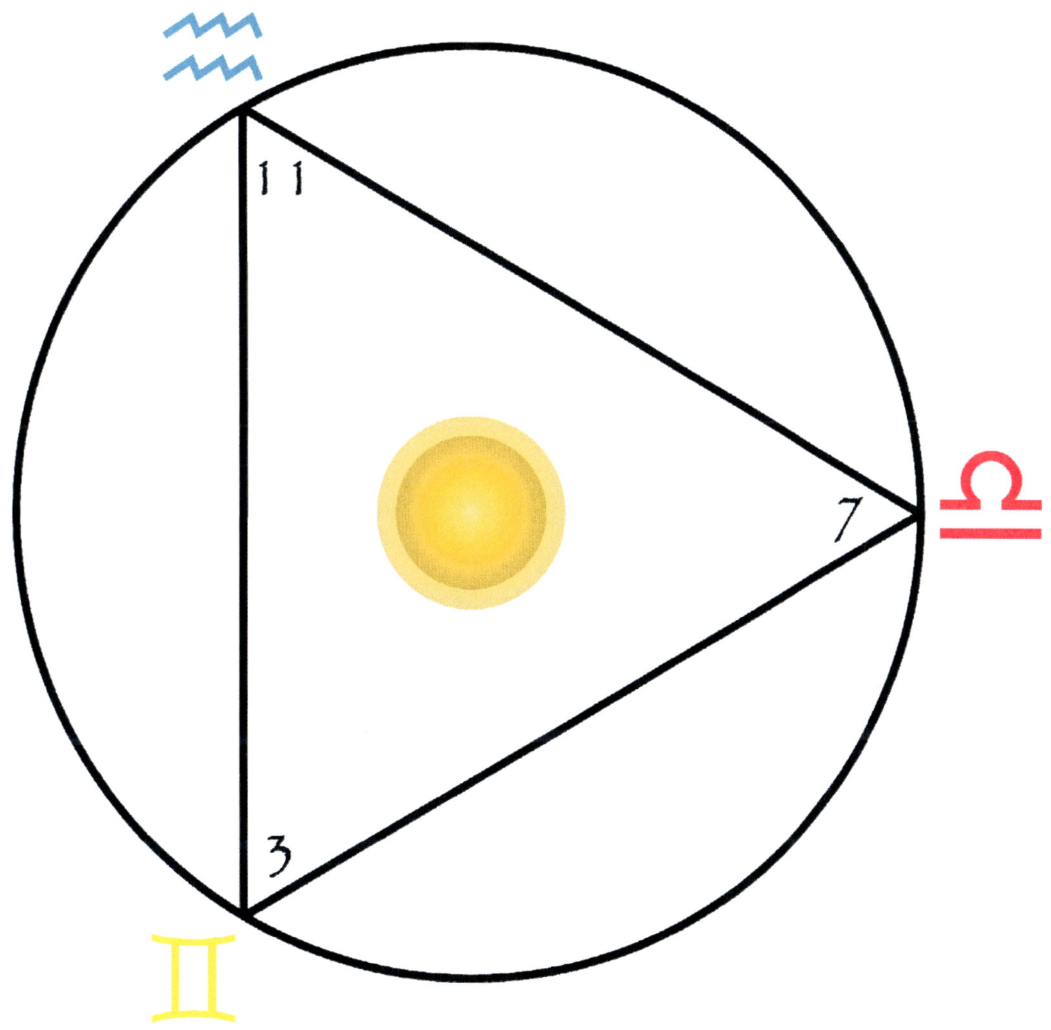

The Signs of the Water Family Pisces, Cancer and Scorpio are reflective, sensitive and intense. Water signs like to nurture and protect.

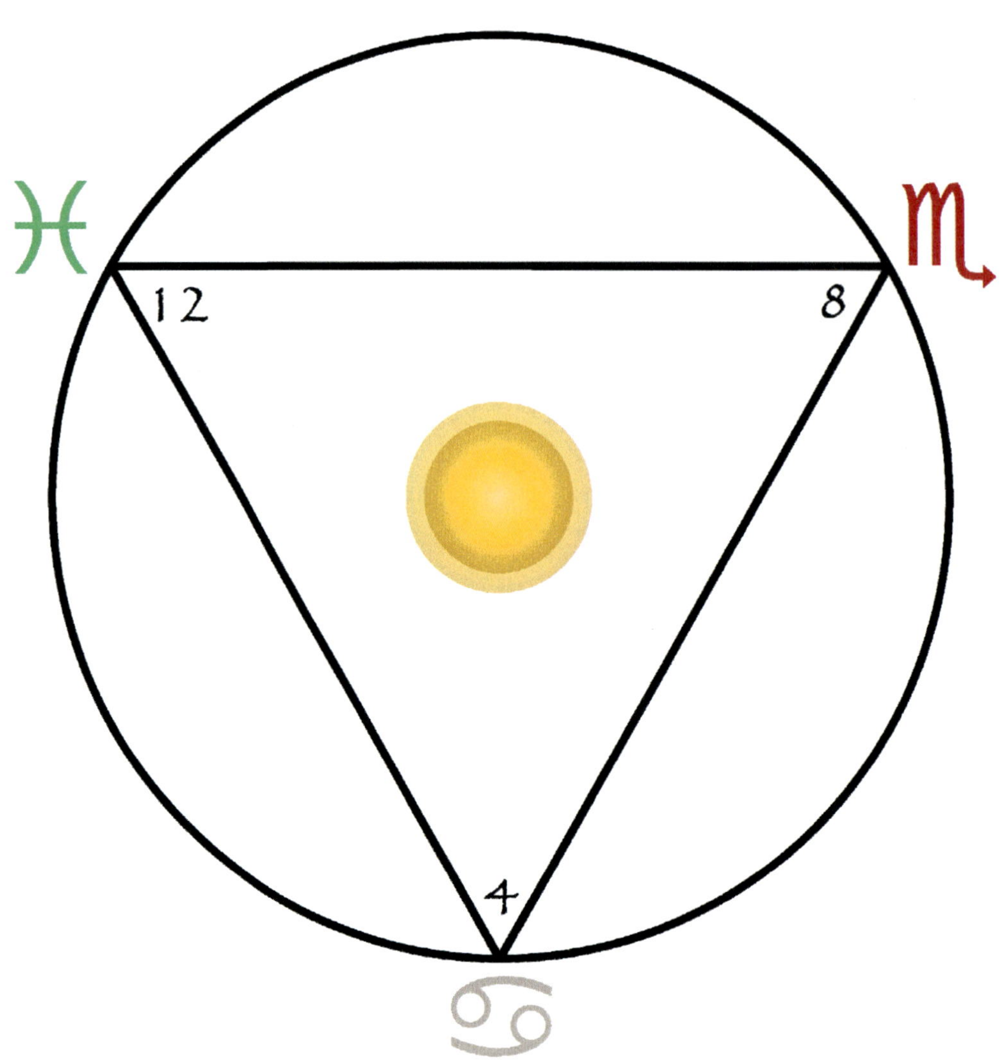

This is what the family of elements Fire, Air, Water and Earth look like in the Astro Neighborhood.

Aries, Capricorn, Cancer and Libra are all Cardinal signs. Cardinal signs mark the beginning of things. Cardinal signs mark the start of the seasons.

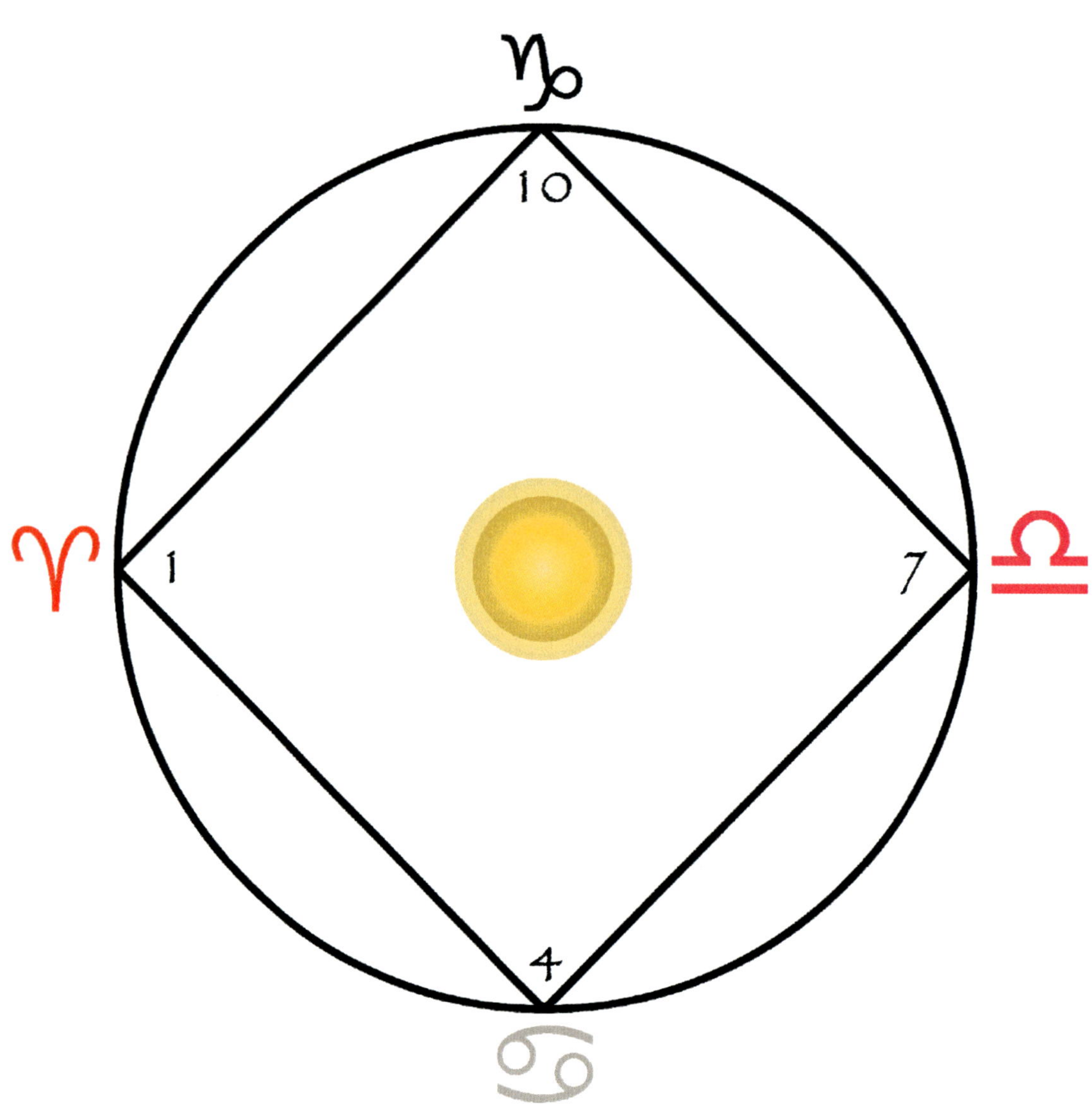

Aquarius, Taurus, Leo and Scorpio are Fixed signs.
Fixed signs are the signs of consistency and persistence!
Fixed signs are focused and great at getting things done.

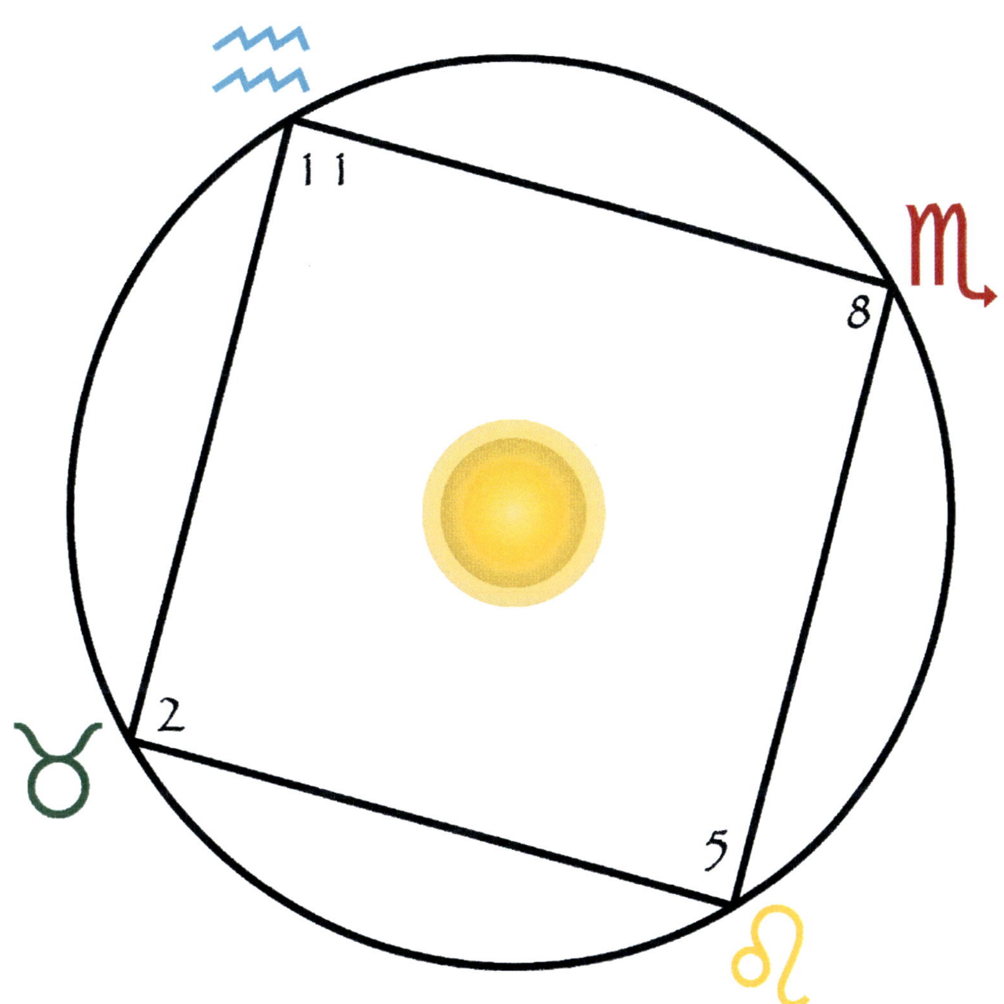

Pisces, Gemini, Virgo and Sagittarius are Mutable signs.
Mutable signs are flexible and shifting.
Mutable signs embrace change and go with the flow.

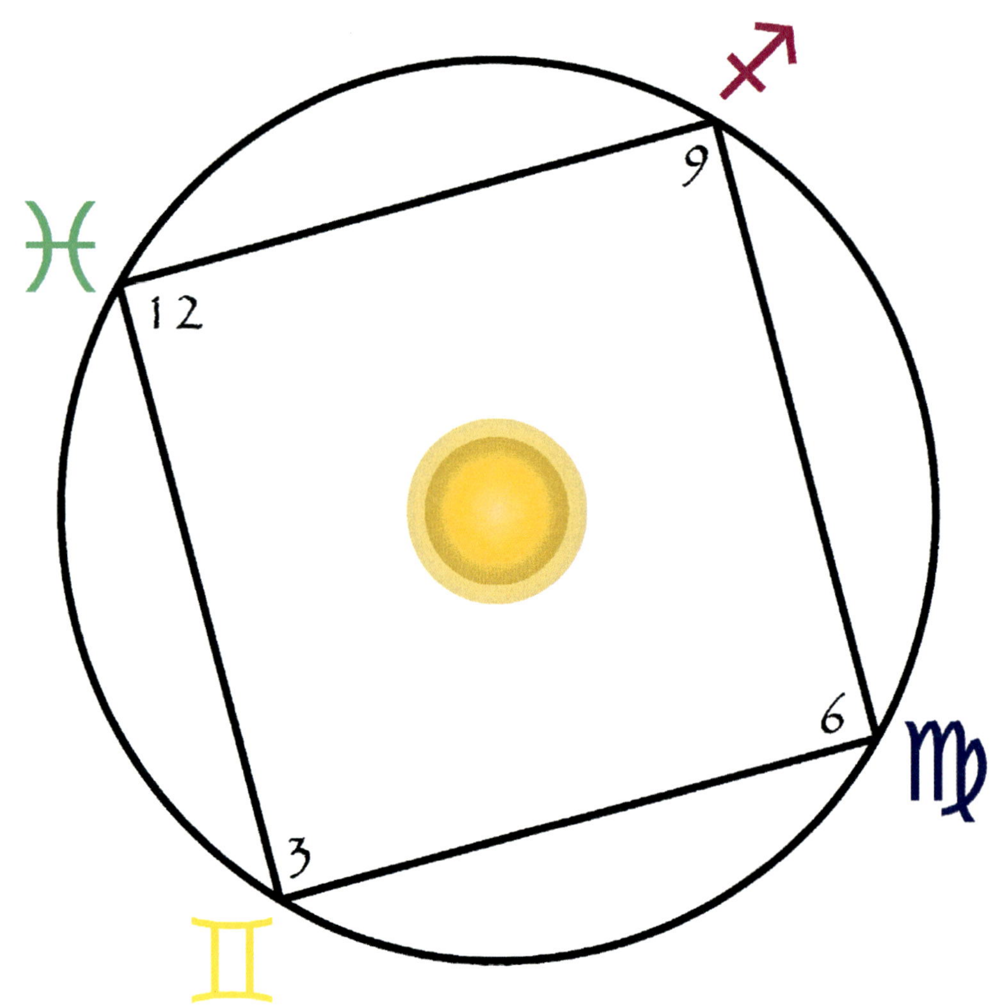

This is what the sign Qualities Cardinal, Mutable and Fixed look like in the Astro Neighborhood.

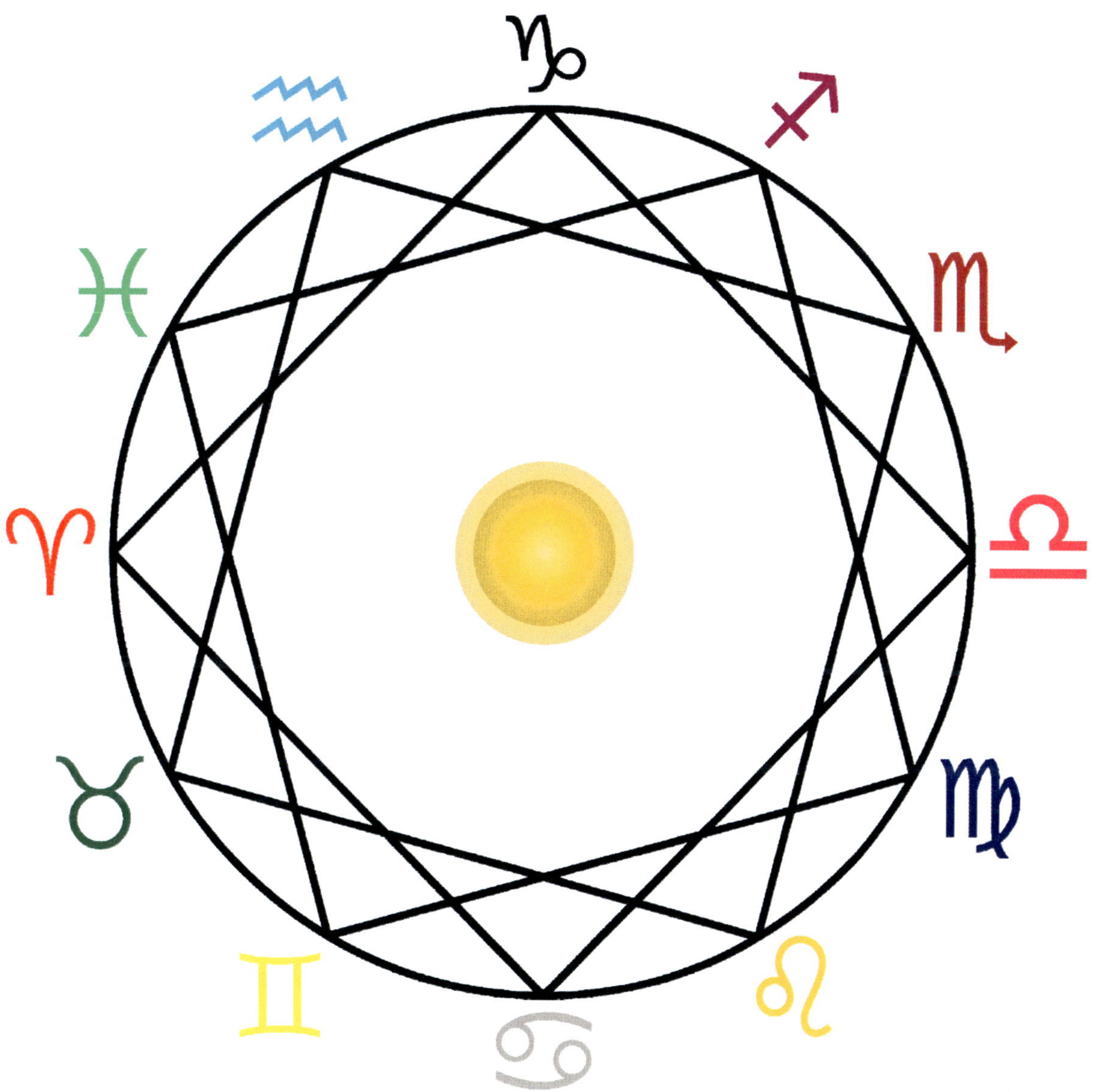

Aries Lives in the 1st House.
Aries is the Cardinal member of the Fire family.
Aries loves themselves!
Aries likes competition and taking action.
Aries connects to the Head of the body.

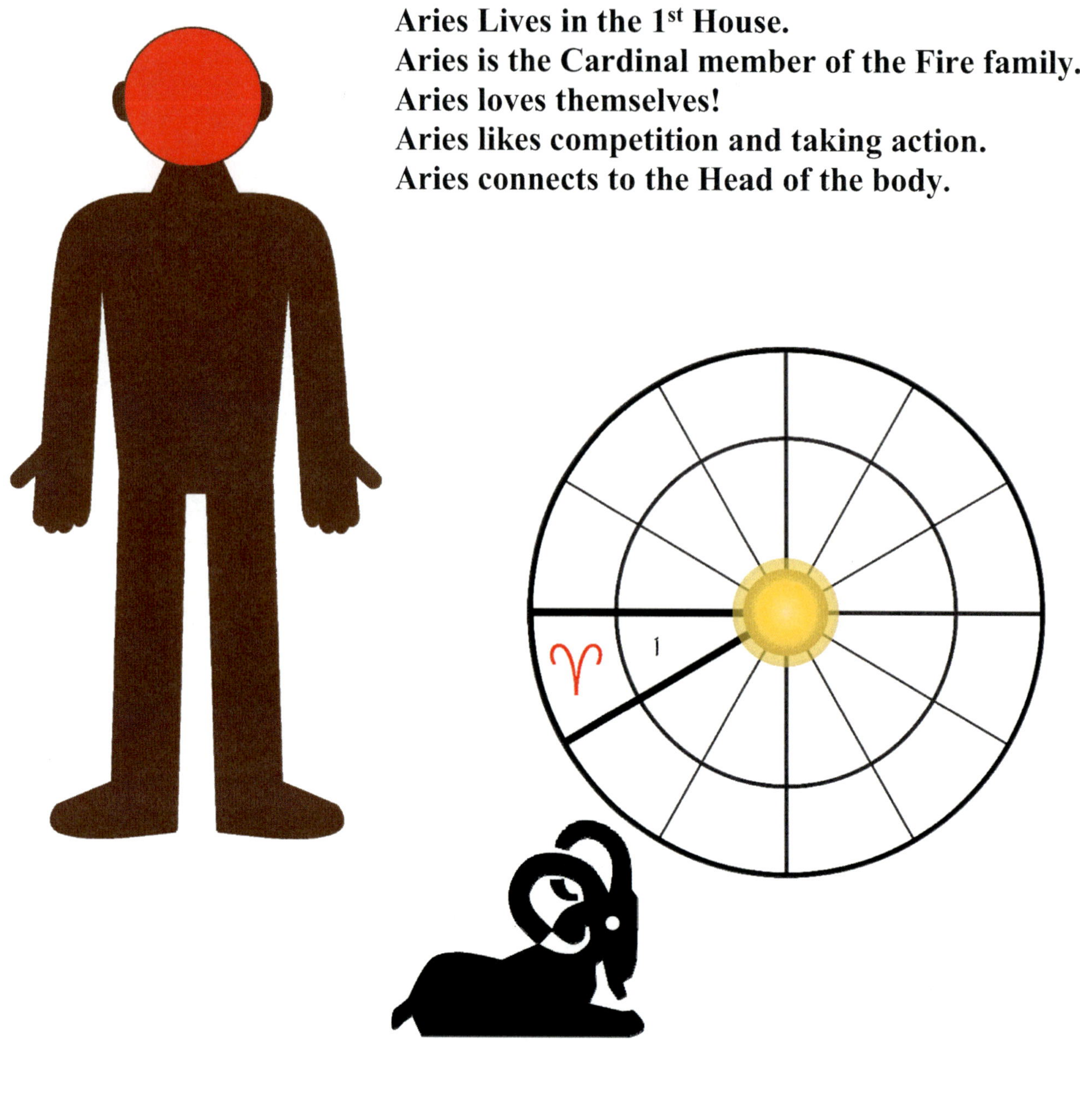

Taurus lives in the 2nd House.
Taurus is the Fixed member of the Earth family.
Taurus likes beautiful things and good food.
Taurus connects to Neck and Ears of the body.

Gemini lives in the 3rd House.
Gemini is the Mutable member of the Air family.
Gemini like to talk and share ideas.
Gemini connect to the Arms and Hands of the body.

Cancer lives in the 4th House.
Cancer is the Cardinal member of the Water family.
Cancer loves to protect and care for others.
Cancer connects to the Chest and Ribs of the body.

Leo lives in the 5th House.
Leo is the Fixed member of the Fire family.
Leo likes to show off and have fun.
Leo connects to the Heart of the body.

Virgo lives in 6th House.
Virgo is the Mutable member of the Earth family.
Virgo likes to work and keeping things tidy.
Virgo connects the Stomach and Small Intestines of the body.

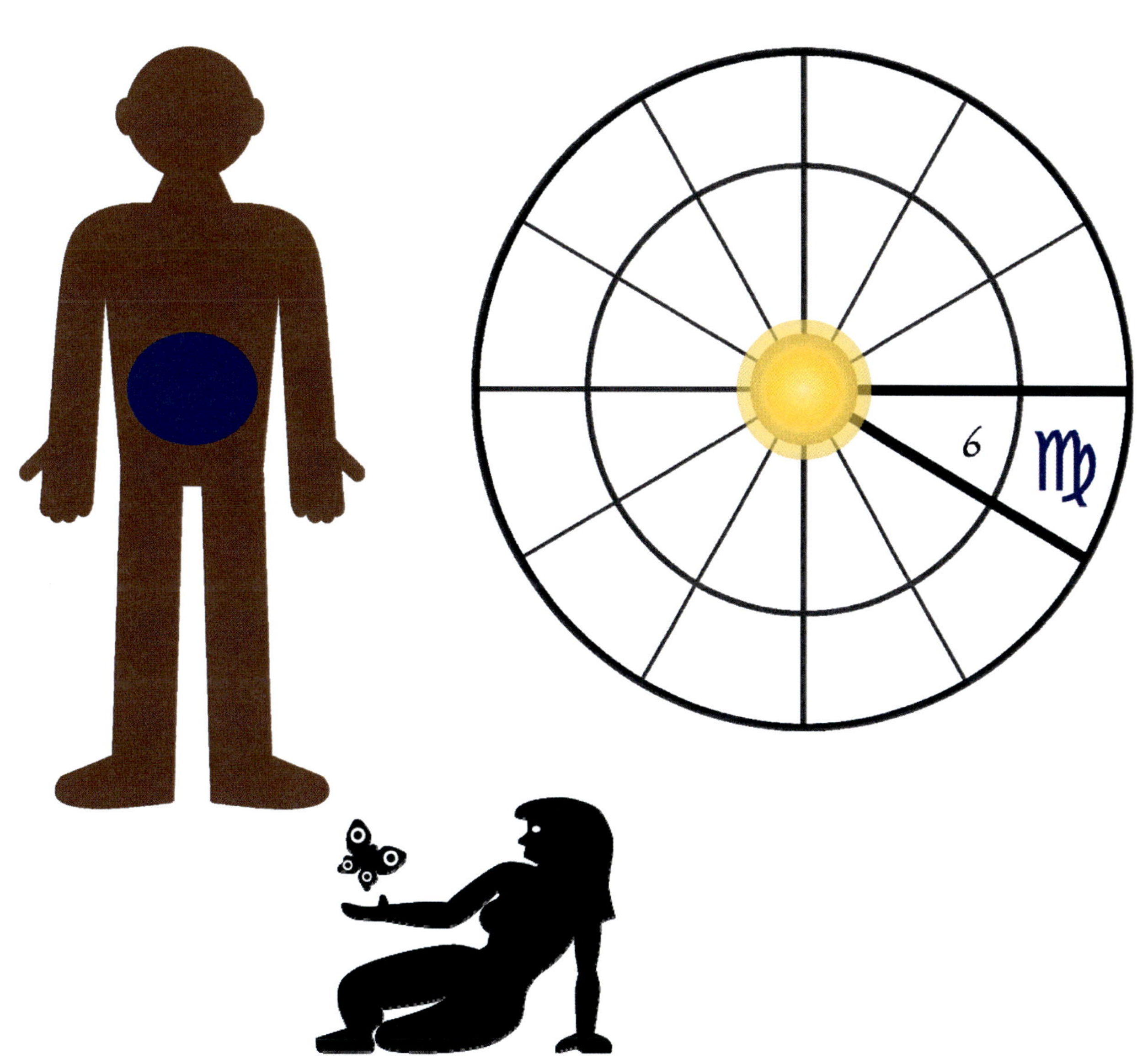

Libra lives in the 7th House.
Libra is the Cardinal member of the Air family.
Libra likes peace and teamwork.
Libra connects to the Kidneys and Lower Back of the body.

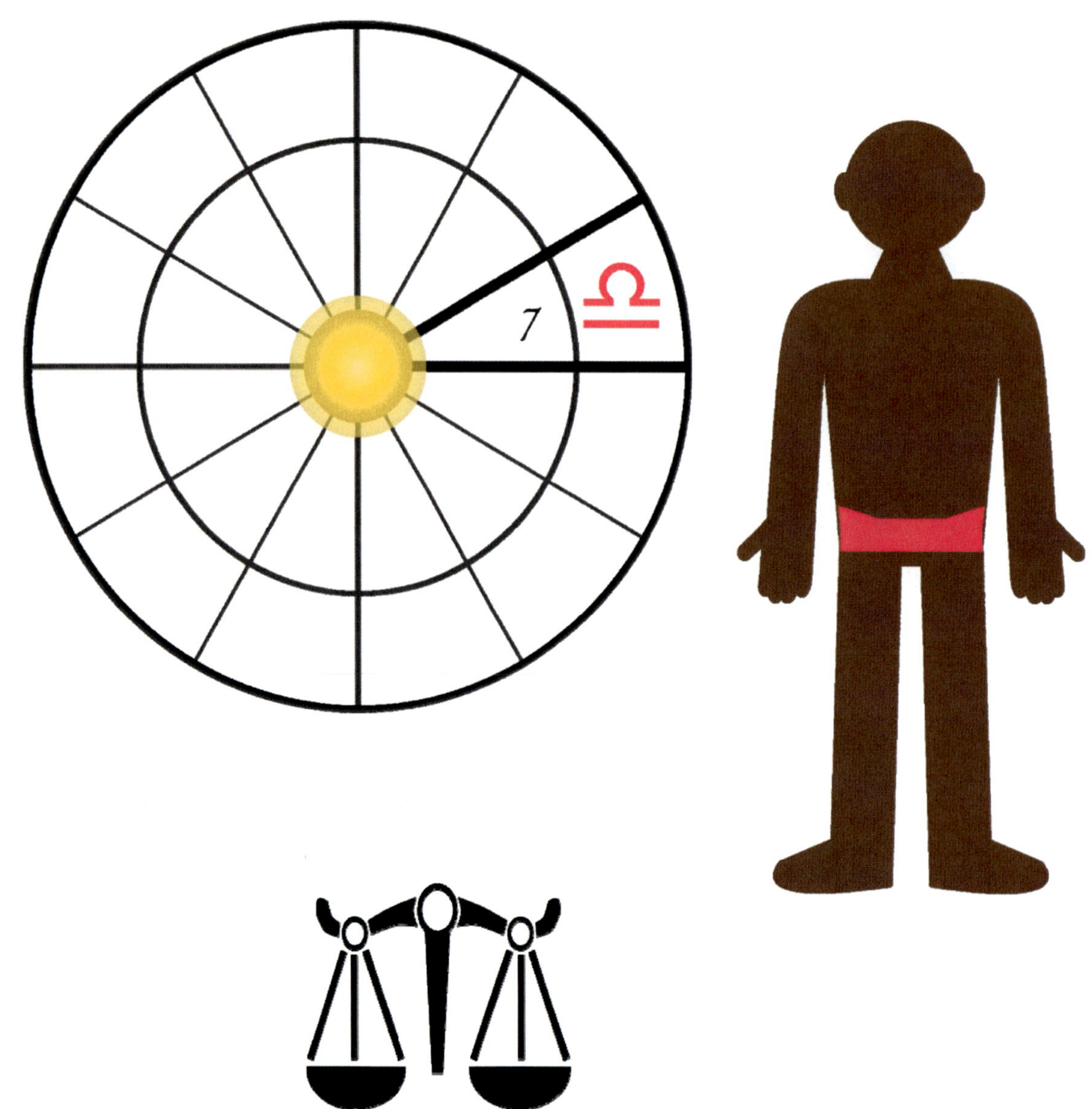

Scorpio lives in the 8th House.
Scorpio is the Fixed member of the Water family. Scorpios likes sharing and transforming. Scorpio connects to the Private parts of the body.

Sagittarius lives in the 9th House.
Sagittarius is the Mutable member of the Fire family.
Sagittarius likes learning and traveling.
Sagittarius connects to the Thighs of the body.

Capricorn lives in the 10th House. Capricorn is the Cardinal member of the Earth family. Capricorn likes order and respect. Capricorns connects to the Bones in the body.

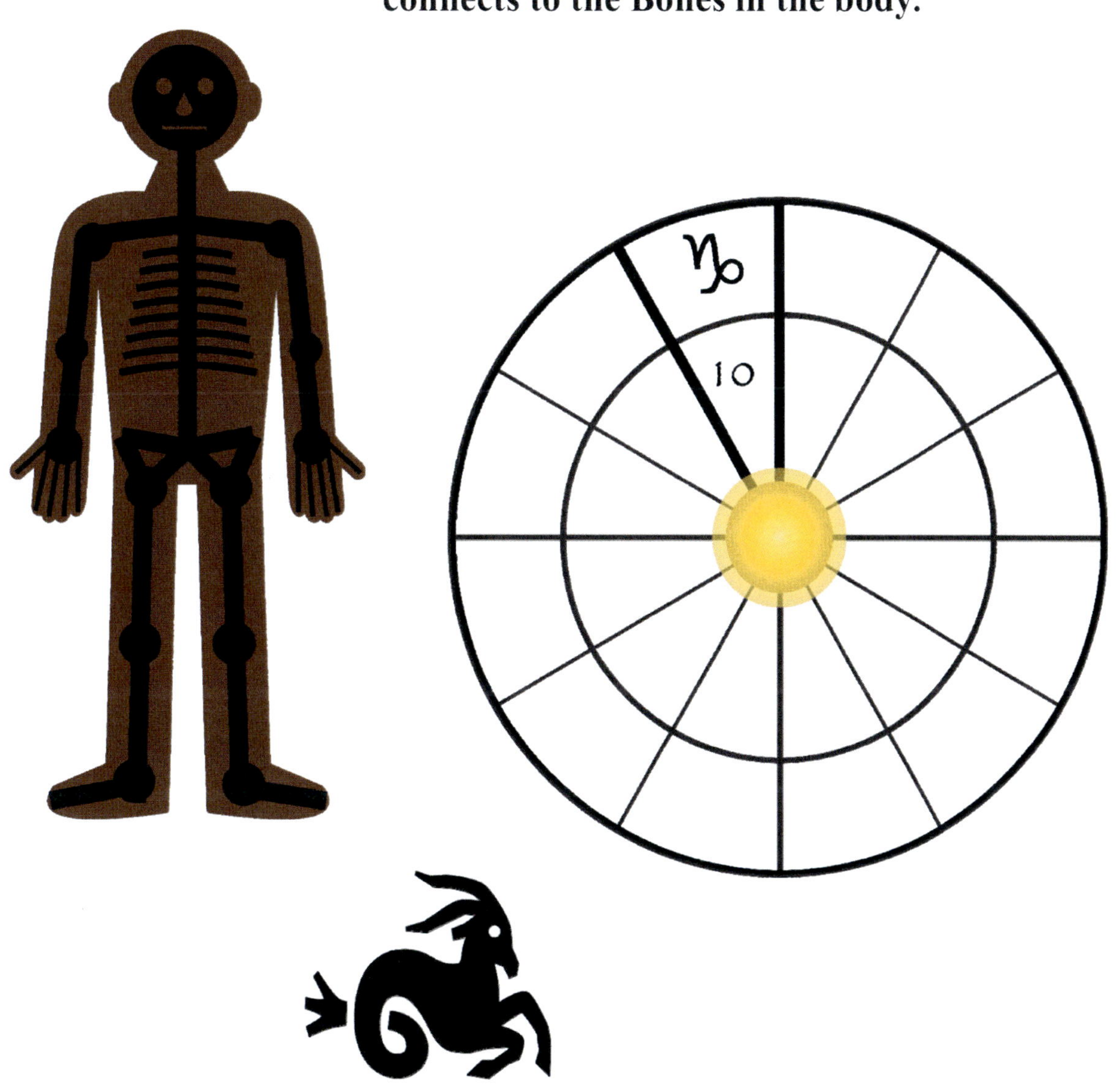

Aquarius lives in the 11th House.
Aquarius is the Fixed member Air Family.
Aquarius likes freedom and being different.
Aquarius connects to the ankles of the body.

Pisces live in the 12th House.
Pisces is the Mutable member of the Water family.
Pisces likes music and fantasy.
Pisces connects to the feet of the body

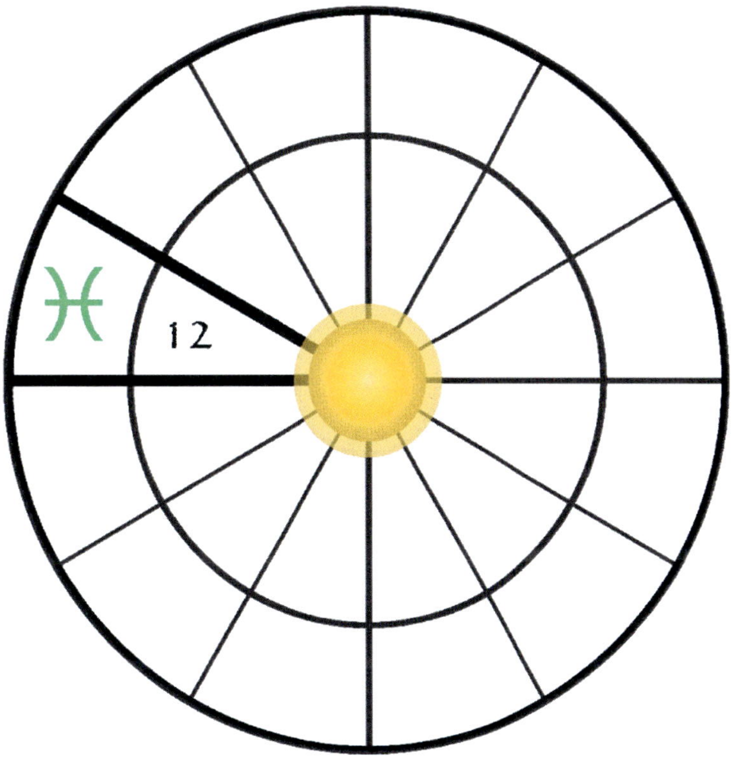

♓ 12

Astrology tells a great story of the Signs and Planets and how we connect to the Universe.
It helps us to understand each other's differences and similarities.
Everyone's birthday is unique and makes them special.
There is no one like YOU on earth!
The way the stars align for you, is just for YOU!

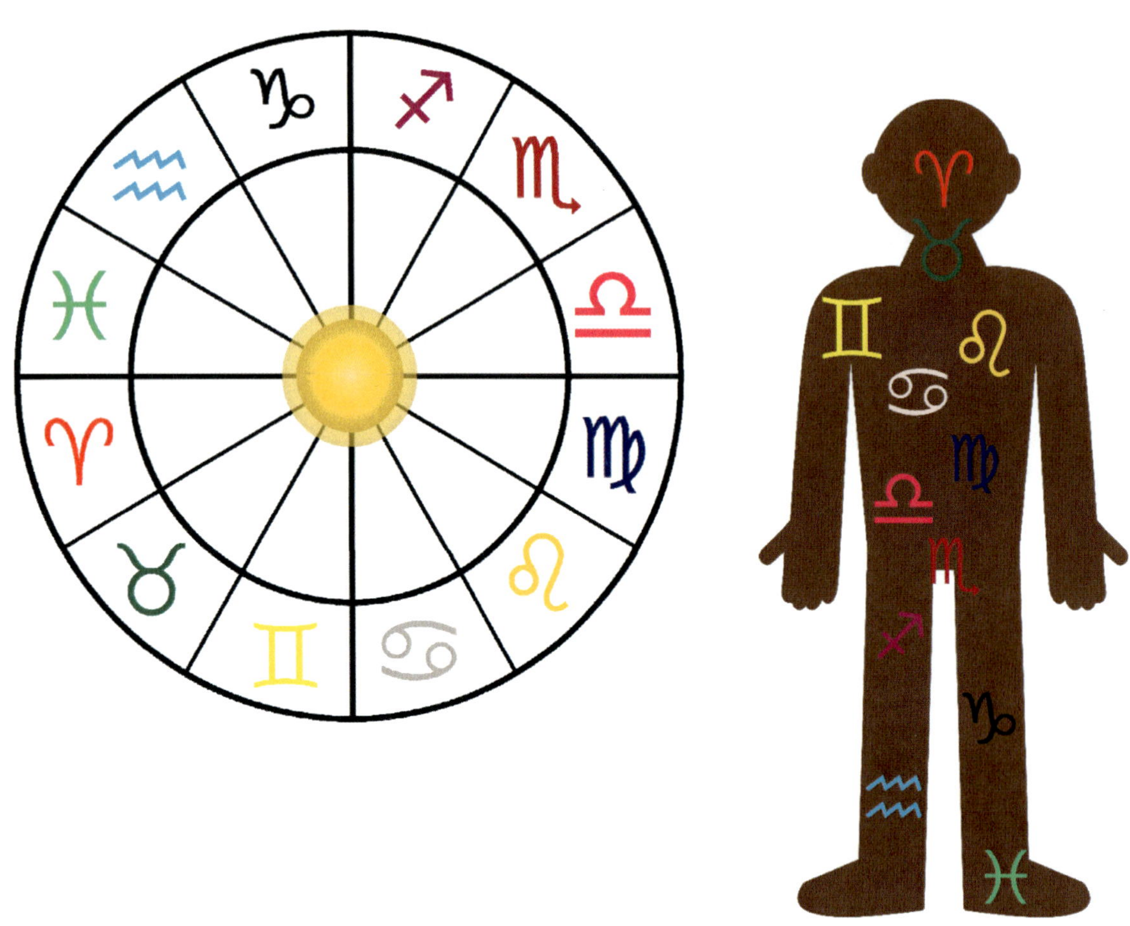

lordsofthepivot.com
IG: Lords_of_the_Pivot FB: Lordsof ThePivot
lordsofthepivot@gmail.com

Made in the USA
Middletown, DE
26 January 2025

69991253R00015